Settings and Cliffhangers

by Martin Waddell

Contents

Section 1
Skinny and Boney	2
It's a Man. United School …	8

Section 2
Someone	12
Dark Night on the Lake	16

Section 3
A Small Problem	22
Zapperjack	26

Edinburgh Gate
Harlow, Essex

Skinny and Boney

The Museum had closed. All the staff had gone home. The cleaners had been and gone and now no one was left in the Museum. The only noise was the buzz of the drinks machine.

It needed fixing after what Knocker and Percy and Sandra had done to it when Miss Clements wasn't looking.

Something stirred in the Bone Room.

It was Skinny.

"I don't like being laughed at," he said. "Those school kids wouldn't laugh at me and call me a stupid bag-of-bones if they knew who I really am."

"Who are you?" Boney said.

"I don't know," said Skinny.

"You don't know because you have no brain," Boney said, sadly.

"I bet I *am* famous," said Skinny. "I must be famous, or I wouldn't have ended up in this glass case. You must be too, because you are in here with me."

"Yes. That's right! Me too! I must be famous as well!" gasped Boney, sounding pleased. He had never thought of it before. Being famous sounded interesting.

"I might be Napoleon, or King Charles ... the one that got his head cut off," said Skinny.

"You can't be King Charles ... you've still got a head," Boney pointed out. "Well, you've got your skull, anyway. And it is still fixed to your neck."

"Maybe they put me together again, after they cut my head off," Skinny said.

"Maybe," said Boney. "But your neck looks okay to me."

Skinny smiled. He *liked* the idea of being a king. It made up for being called a stupid bag-of-bones by the Dawn Street School kids. Napoleon would have been all right too. Knocker and Sandra wouldn't have dared call Napoleon a stupid bag-of-bones. Percy wouldn't have stuck his Man. U. sticker on Napoleon's glass case either.

"I don't like being laughed at. I'm going to go and find out who we are," said Skinny, sitting up. He opened the lid of their glass case, and climbed out.

"Wait for me!" Boney said, and he climbed out after Skinny. They rattled a bit when they moved, as skeletons do. Their knees and elbows were a bit stiff, because of the wires that held the bones together.

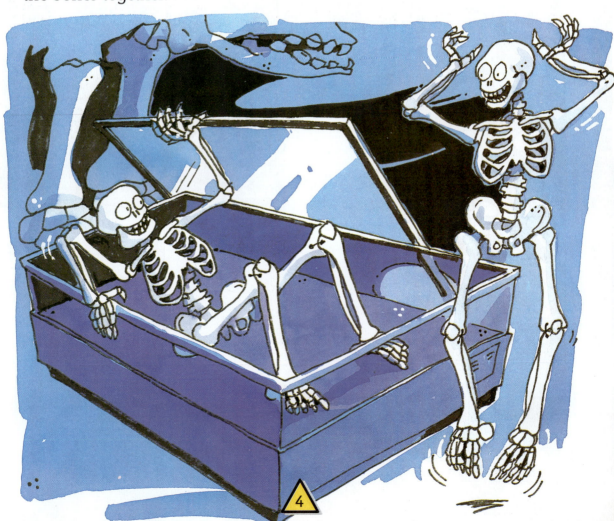

"Don't go!" said the Dinosaur next to the door, as they headed toward him.

"If you go we'll have no one to talk to," said the Brontosaurus.

"Sorry guys, but we're off to find out who we are," Boney explained.

They went down the corridor, past the drinks machine to the staff cloakroom. There they each picked up a coat and a hat. The Museum was always warm, and they knew it would be cold outside.

They went out into Web Lane.

"Evening paper, Sir?" said the paper seller and then he went AAAAAAAAAAAAAAAAAAAAAAAAAAAAAAAAAH! and ran away.

"He didn't laugh at us," said Skinny, proudly.

"He was too frightened," said Boney. They rattled on down Web Lane.

"What's your game, gents?" said the policeman. He had heard the strange rattling as they went past him. "I'll have your names and addresses."

"Skinny," said Skinny.

"And Boney," said Boney.

"But those are not our real names," said Skinny.

"We don't know our real names because we have no brains," said Boney. And they took their hats off to show him.

The policeman went
AAAAAAAAAAAAAAAAAAAAAAAAAAAAAH!
and ran away.

"Scaredy Custard!" said Skinny, putting his hat back on.

That's when Knocker came dashing round the corner, with Sandra and Percy after him. Knocker was waving Sandra's schoolbag round his head and yelling.

Knocker came to a dead stop.

"Oooooo-er!" he gasped, going pale. The two skeletons came rattling toward him, grinning toothless grins, their white leg-bones showing beneath their flapping coats …

It's a Man. United School …

"Docky? Docky? We've got to do something Docky, or there's going to be a lot of bother," Jan said. They were on the way to school, but they'd stopped off in the park at the far end of the Estate. Jan had *made* Docky go there, because she wanted to talk to him.

Docky was sitting on the roof of the burned-out car. Someone had dumped it on the grassy patch of mud behind the swings. The car was a good look-out place. Sitting on it, he could spot anyone coming who might be trouble. That meant Tony Minton.

"I don't have to do anything," Docky said. "Not a single thing. It's got nothing to do with me. Nothing to do with you either, Jan. It's not our fault that Bernard's a stupid Everton fan, is it?"

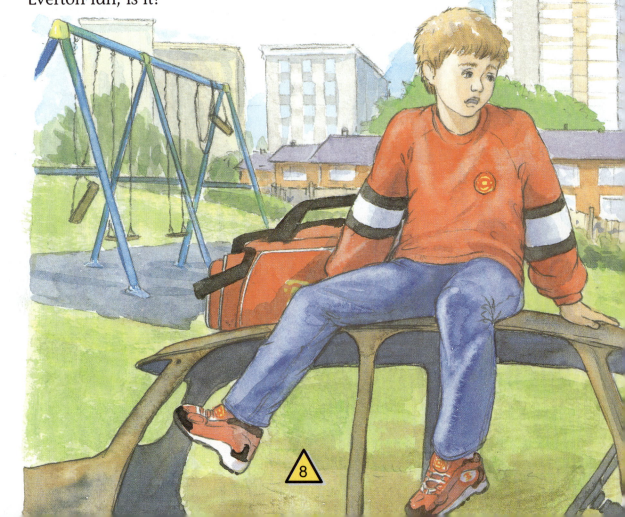

"This isn't only about Bernard," Jan said. "Not just him. It's about what's happened to the whole school. The way Tony Minton and his Man. United Fan Club have taken everything over."

"Yes, well. I've got myself to look after," Docky muttered, turning his head away.

"What are you scared of?" Jan said. "Why don't you stand up to Tony?"

"I don't go *looking* for trouble, do I?" Docky said.

Jan thought she would try tackling him another way.

"You don't *really* support Man. United, do you Docky?" she began. "You used to support Notts. Forest before you came to our school. Your mum told my mum you had Forest kit when you went to that other school. And you had Forest stuff all over the walls of your bedroom. When you came to our school you took it all down and made her get you Man. United stuff instead, didn't you?"

"That was then. Man. United's the best team now, aren't they?" Docky said, sounding uneasy.

"Man. United win everything and they are always on TV. So they must be good. And everyone supports them. Even the teachers. Mr Parks does, and it is his school. He's Man. United. Everybody is."

"Everybody except poor Bernard," Jan said. "He's Everton. That's his team."

"Bernard was *warned*," Docky said, grimly. "We told him, first day he came. He knows it's a Man. United school. He shouldn't come here if he isn't United. No one supports Everton here. Everton are rubbish. Mr Parks says so too. Mr Parks set up our Man. United Fan Club for us. And our web site. And Mr Parks is going to fix it so we get to a Man. United game next term. Maybe it will be against Everton. Man. United will beat them hollow."

"It would be tough for Bernard," Jan said. "All of you kids and Mr Parks yelling for United against his team."

"Bernard can stay home if he doesn't fancy it," Docky said, with a grin.

"That's nice. That's really friendly," Jan said. "Poor little kid. His dad dies. His mum moves down here. He is dumped in a new school. He turns up at school first day in the Everton blue that his dad got him. And that's how he gets greeted."

"Bernard's stupid dad should have got Bernard a Man. United kit like everyone else," Docky said.

"You're mean, Docky," Jan said. "Talking about Bernard's dad like that." She went off, and Docky trailed along behind her.

They came down the hill, toward the school gates. Tony Minton and his mates were waiting there in their Man. United gear. They were laughing and joking with each other.

Bernard came toward them, all alone. He was wearing his blue Everton gear. He'd hung about as long as he could, but now the bell was about to ring. He had to go in, past his enemies. Bernard looked as if he wanted to run away, but he didn't. He hitched his badly ripped Everton bag up on his shoulder and kept on walking.

Jan called, "Bernard! Bernard! Wait for me." Bernard didn't wait. He went on through the gate, head down, looking sicky-scared …

Someone

One time I had an adventure with ghosts, or a ghost anyway. It happened this way.

My dad grazes our sheep miles up on Banagher's mountain, near the old house that used to belong to the McAuleys. In those days it had a fire in the hearth. Now the hearth stone is cold and the house belongs to no one. One winter night we got caught up there, myself and my big brother Sam, and Rio our dog.

Sam and I had climbed a long way that day.

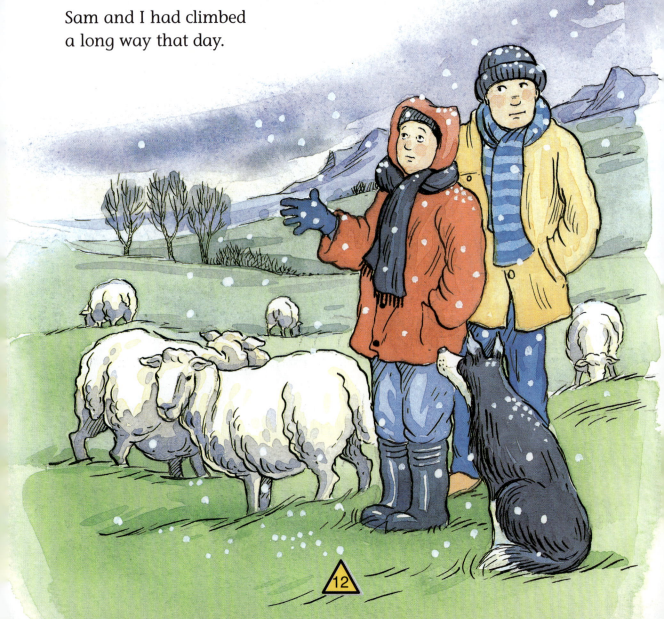

We'd left the
lane above
Huckerby's place,
and followed the path
to the right of the stream. We went over the
water above the tree line and then we had to
climb up the Hare's Leap. Not many people go
there in winter, for no one needs to but us. There is nothing up
there but our sheep. We made our way by the long path round
Slieve Call along the side of the blue lake as far as the cairn.
Then we were out onto the side of Banagher's mountain. We were
there a long time with the sheep, and while we were there, it
started to snow. The man on the TV said there wouldn't be snow
but there was, and quickly the snowing and blowing got worse. It
was nearly a blizzard, blowing bitter and cold in our faces.

"It's no use, Tom," Sam said. "Dad always says we're not to go
down when the snow has a grip." We made for the house that
had once belonged to the McAuleys.

There isn't much of a house left now. It has four walls, a roof made of slate and an old door that's half off its hinges. My dad keeps things there for sleeping and eating, and making a fire, for he's been caught out on the mountain often enough. The place was soon cosy and warm, although it was bitter outside. We were just fine by the fire.

Rio was lying by Sam's feet. Suddenly, his head went up and his ears pricked.

"Rio?" Sam said, looking down at the dog. "What's up?" Rio got to his feet and padded past us, circling away from the fire, towards the door.

He stopped a few feet from it, dropping down on his belly. He's half collie, half springer, and that's how they behave when there is something to watch. They are grand dogs for working with sheep.

"What's wrong with him?" Sam said.

"Search me," I said.

"Rio?" Sam said. "Rio. Come here." Rio wouldn't come, and that's not like him. He is a working dog, and does what he's told. Sam is the one the dog works with, so Rio always obeys … but this time, he didn't.

"Here, boy, here," Sam said, getting to his feet. Rio looked around him, but his head turned back immediately. He held his head to one side, eyes gleaming. He wasn't frightened, just interested. He looked the way he looks when he's watching a fly on the window, and wondering if he can catch it. He'd be all day at that game if we let him.

That's when it happened.

Rio stood up and bounced forward, wagging his tail.

"Look Sam," I said slowly. "Look *there!*" There was someone else in the room, someone who certainly wasn't like Sam or me for we are solid and can't be seen through … not like the someone who was now in the room.

Dark Night on the Lake

Dad said I should take Martina down the lake on the *Katie D.*, fishing. I suppose he thought that that would stop us quarrelling, but it didn't.

"We'll go in the narrow channels between the reeds," I told Martina.

"Okay, if you want to," she said. "Please yourself. You always do."

Martina didn't fish. I did, but she didn't. She sat there looking grumpy. I didn't pay her much attention. The worst of it was that I got so interested in what I was doing that I lost my sense of direction. Soon I hadn't a clue where I was, or what direction I should be going. We were lost in the maze of the reed channels and the light was fading, fast.

"I'm not enjoying myself. I want to go home now, please," Martina said.

"In a minute," I said.

"*Now,*" she said.

"We *are* going home," I said. Well, I hoped we were anyway, but I was beginning to have my doubts. The reed channels are a bad place to be lost in, after dark. You can't see anything except the sky, because of the height of the reeds. The channels are narrow and windy, so it is difficult to work out exactly where you are.

"Why don't you use the outboard engine?" Martina asked.

"We can't," I told her. "The water is too shallow. Anyone with any sense would know that."

"Would you like me to take a turn rowing?" Martina asked, pretending to be helpful.

"I want to get home tonight," I told her.

"Are you saying I *can't row*?" she said.

"I'm saying I'm better at it. I've been rowing round here most of my life," I told her.

"So what? I may not *do* boats like you, but I can manage an oar as well as any boy," she said hugging her arms.

She was up in the bow end of the boat, hunched up and shivering. She'd come out in a stupid T-shirt, and now the cold was getting to her.

"It is my fault we are in this mess, so I'm going to get us out of it," I told her. "Just let me get on with it, okay?"

"You mean you've got us lost," she said.

"Well … sort of," I admitted.

"Why can't we turn round and go back the way we came?" she asked. "That's what I'd do."

If I had known which way we'd come we wouldn't have been lost. North, South, East or West, I hadn't a clue which way we were headed.

"We made too many twists and turns when we were fishing," I said. "If I had a compass I could do it, but I haven't."

"Row toward the moon," Martina suggested. "It was rising behind us when we started out, so if we can work our way back toward it we should be okay." Maybe she was smarter than she looked.

It got even darker and colder, and we seemed to find our way further into the reed channels, in spite of all my attempts to get us out. We rowed in and out, in and out and in and out, getting nowhere. We were still doing it when the *Katie D.* bumped against something. The boat rocked, and came to a sudden stop.

"We must be stuck in the mud," I said.

"No, we're not," Martina said. "We've hit a rock or something sticking up out of the water."

"There aren't any rocks here, just mud," I told her. "Anyone with any sense would know that."

"We hit *something*," she insisted. Martina moved down the boat, and reached out with her right arms for the something.

"It's beneath the surface of the water," she reported. "That is what you bumped into. It's a package of some sort. It is tied to a marker float and there is another float at the other end. The package is wrapped in plastic, and bound up with tape. It's round, like a wheel … quite big."

"Funny place to hide something," I said. "Nobody ever comes here."

"That's why the place was chosen," Martina said, and then she grinned and added, "*Anyone with any sense would know that.*"

Kneeling in the boat, she pulled the package out of the water …

A Small Problem

There was a squeal and a hiss and then …

… a tiny *something* dashed out of the Head Teacher's room, heading for the Old Store. The *something* was headed for the Store because no one ever went there anymore. The Old Store was where it was safest to be.

Tinker the school cat came belting out after the *something*. After Tinker came a panic-stricken Duggie, trying to put right his worst-ever mistake.

Down the corridor, past Year Three and the boys' toilets ran the *something*, and Tinker, and Duggie, in that order.

Round the corner, past Year Two and Year One and Reception Year ran the something, and Tinker, and Duggie, in that order.

In through the open door of the Old Store ran the *something*. Tinker and Duggie followed, in that order … and that's when the *something* disappeared.

Tinker couldn't see it, and Duggie couldn't see it, but *it* could see *them* looking for it.

Tinker sat down and started inspecting one of her front paws. Duggie stood very still, looking round him.

Tinker got up and stalked round the Store, the tip of her tail flicking.

"Clear off, cat!" Duggie muttered. Nobody else was there, which was lucky for Duggie. Big kids weren't allowed anywhere near the Reception Year corridor, let alone the Old Store. Duggie didn't want to get caught where he wasn't supposed to be, but he couldn't go off without sorting things out either.

Tinker looked at him, her green eyes glittering. She stalked toward the door on soft paws. Now the hunt was over, she was changing back into the tame old purry lap-cat that the dinner ladies fussed over.

Duggie followed her to the door, just to be sure she was going. He watched carefully until the cat had disappeared back down the corridor, heading for the kitchens, and her saucer of milk. He knew just what the *something* was, even if Tinker didn't.

The door of the green cupboard was slightly open. That didn't surprise Duggie one bit. He opened the door wider, and looked inside.

"Mr Smithers?" he whispered. "Don't be frightened, Mr Smithers." There was no reply.

"It's me, Mr Smithers," Duggie said raising his voice. There was still no reply.

"Mr Smithers?" said Duggie. "There's no need to be scared anymore. Tinker's gone. You can come out now. It is quite safe. Honest. The cat's gone, and she won't be coming back." Still no reply.

"This is stupid, Mr Smithers. I know you are in there," Duggie said, beginning to lose his patience.

Then …

"Are you sure that cat's gone?" said a shaky voice, from somewhere near the back of the cupboard where it was darkest.

"Is that you, Mr Smithers?" Duggie asked anxiously.

"It *might* be," said the voice, carefully, not giving anything away.

"You can come out now," Duggie said. "I promise you the cat's gone."

"Close the door of the room first, so Tinker can't get back in," the voice said, sounding nervous … "I'm not risking that again." Duggie crossed the room, closed the door softly, and came back to the cupboard.

"Is there anyone else here?" the voice asked. "Anyone else with great clumping feet who might decide to stand on me by mistake?"

"Only me," Duggie said. "You're quite safe."

"Right," said the voice. "It is time we got this sorted. You shrunk me, Duggie Morton. If it wasn't for you I'd still be my usual size. I'm supposed to be the Head Teacher round here, not something the cat chases. It's *your* fault that I'm the size I am now. You got me into this mess, and you can get me out, pronto, or else …"

Zapperjack

Suddenly, Jack wasn't in his bedroom sitting at his game-table, where he had been the moment before.

He should have been there, but he wasn't.

"This just doesn't happen!" Jack thought, but he was too excited to be frightened.

He had been in his bedroom when he pressed F1, and entered in his personal password, ZAPPERJACK. All he had done was follow the instructions that came with the game and then … then he *wasn't* in his room, playing with his computer.

He was somewhere else, somewhere entirely different from his bedroom, somewhere cold and dark and dangerous.

"There's only one place this *can* be!" he told himself. He was in his new computer game, the Monster Maze. The instructions had said he would be, and now he was. The force-field shield that he had selected from the Set-up Menu before he started playing was beside him. His zapper was still in his hand. He picked up his force-field shield, and moved forward, holding his zapper ready to fire.

"It is dark. I can't see much," Jack thought. "How do I get out of this?" As his eyes got used to the darkness, he could see that he was in a cave. Passages ran out of it, in different directions. The walls were bright red. The floor was covered in mud and something that he guessed must be the dried-up blood of monsters.

"This is the best computer game ever!" Jack decided, then …

bleep-bleep-bleep.

Part of the wall of the cave faded away, in front of his eyes. Where it had been, there was a huge screen. It was dark blue, and as Jack watched a message came up, printing one letter at a time, as though the Maze Master was tapping it onto a keyboard, for Jack's benefit.

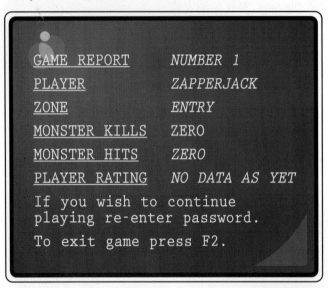

```
GAME REPORT       NUMBER 1
PLAYER            ZAPPERJACK
ZONE              ENTRY
MONSTER KILLS     ZERO
MONSTER HITS      ZERO
PLAYER RATING     NO DATA AS YET
If you wish to continue
playing re-enter password.
To exit game press F2.
```

Quickly, Jack tapped his ZAPPERJACK password on the panel of his zapper. The screen flickered, briefly, and the printing started all over again.

```
PLAY LEVEL SELECTION MENU
1 BEGINNER
2 TRAINEE
3 MAZE MAN
4 MAZE COMMANDER
5 MAZE LEADER
```

"Maze Leader means me!" Jack decided at once, and he tapped in 5 on his zapper.

There was a warning bleep-bleep-bleep sound, and a new message appeared, tapped out one letter at a time.

WARNING! WARNING! WARNING!

The Play Level you have selected is Highly Dangerous. AS A NEW PLAYER IN THE MONSTER MAZE YOU ARE ADVISED TO SELECT A LOWER SKILL LEVEL.

Press F1 to return to menu.

Re-enter password to continue.

Jack grinned and tapped in his ZAPPERJACK password again on his zapper. If the kids at school heard that he had started *any* game at a lower skill level they just wouldn't believe it. He *had* to select Level 5. He hadn't any choice. Jack hadn't won his title as Keyboard King of Twine Street School by starting off at Level 2 or 3. Low levels were for little kids.

The big screen started to shiver and shake and then there were three short beeps

beep-beep-beep

followed by a loud blaring sound.

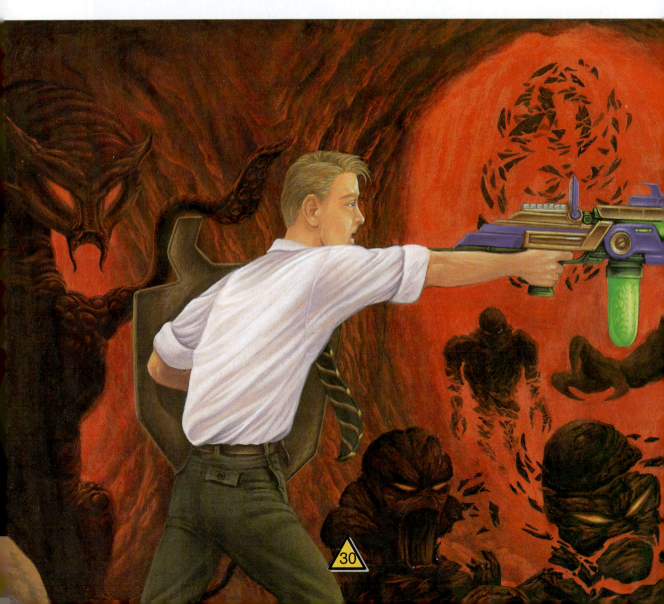

The screen with the words on it disappeared, leaving Jack alone in the Monster Maze.

"GAME ON!" Jack shouted, waving his zapper.

Suddenly, dark shapes were moving all around him, coming out of the passages of the Maze. Jack raised his zapper and fired **zap-zap-zap**.

The Maze Monsters were blown to pieces. Little bits of them floated about in the air, and came down around Jack. Then the little pieces started making themselves back into more Maze Monsters.

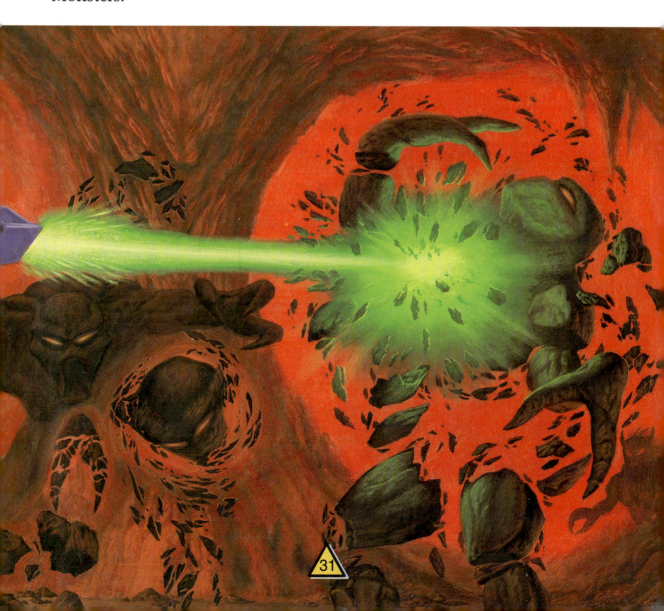

Jack had guessed that might happen, but he hadn't time to worry about it because out of the floor of the Maze rose a huge Thing. Its red tongue licked out of its mouth, whipping at Jack and driving him back. It had short arms and huge fat legs, and a hard green skin.

"Easy-peasy!" thought Jack, taking aim.

Zap-zap-zap went Jack's zapper but …

zap-zap-

zap-bidddd-dooooooong! The zap struck the Thing's skin, and bounced off it, heading straight back for Jack and

BOOOOOOOOOOOOOOOOOOOOOOM!

Jack was zapped, just like that.

He lay stunned on the floor of the Maze with the Thing hip-hopping toward him. The ground shook each time the Thing moved. Jack's zapper was out of action and his force-field shield was broken and useless.

Then, from nowhere at all, a VOICE boomed through the Maze. "*This is the Maze Master …*"